WHAT DO YOU THINK YOU ARE FEELING?

by Chew Yin Chan

explore with Us and see how we feel.

Curly

monkey

S.I.D

To order additional copies of this book, contact
Toll Free +65 3165 7531 (Singapore)
Toll Free +60 3 3099 4412 (Malaysia)
www.partridgepublishing.com/singapore
orders.singapore@partridgepublishing.com

ISBN
978-1-5437-7454-2 (sc)
978-1-5437-7481-8 (e)

Print information available on the last page.

07/31/2023

PARTRIDGE

previous book....

ADVENTURES WITH...
CURLY & MONKEY

Book 1.   By Chew Yin Chan

.... are you ready to join in with this picture book, exploring feelings? remember there are no right or wrong ways to feel, tell us how you think **Curly** and **monkey** are feeling...

this is **S.I.D**

Curly named **S.I.D** from the badge on S.I.D's chest

S.I.D

Society for Intergalactic Development

S.I.D travels on this spaceship...

MONKEY IS FEELING OK!

S.I.D

...in fact, **monkey** enjoyed the beaming up experience.... it was the nervous feeling he did not enjoy...

...it's OK to feel **nervous**

...and then

OH **NO** ! exclaimed Curly

I'VE LOST GORDON !

Gordon is a small toy giraffe, which Curly treasures

picture of Gordon

...taking 5 deep breaths **monkey** and **Curly**, think of **Gordon**...

is Gordon on the sheep farm...?

...can you see Gordon?

...is Gordon at the beach?

WE CAN ALL BE **THERE** FOR CURLY

monkey is there for **Curly**

How do you think Curly is feeling?

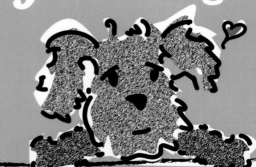

...next minute

SURPRISE!

...what has surprised Curly, monkey and S.I.D?

I'M GLAD GORDON IS STILL OUT THERE!
says **Curly**

Curly is still sad and wishes that Gordon was with them inside the spaceship...

...how do **YOU feel,** knowing Gordon is not lost...?

...over the next several days they follow Gordon in space...

...Gordon is floating around the earth...

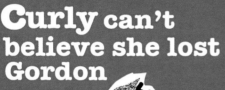

Curly can't believe she lost Gordon

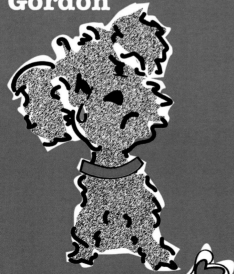

Curly is **angry** that they can't get Gordon back

Curly is **sad**...

Curly has accepted she has lost Gordon.
...every now and then Curly will think of her cherished buddy...
maybe when they return to space the friends will see
Gordon again.

... for now it's
time to take
a trip to earth

Earth

WHERE SHALL
WE VISIT ON
EARTH?

S.I.D

.... do you think **you** can remember
the different feelings in this book?

S.I.D   **Curly**   **monkey**

saying see you soon...

24

About the author and illustrator:

Chew Yin is a Holistic therapist/ life coach and designer.

Through facilitating the journeys of her clients,

and within her own life experiences, Chew Yin

became aware that expressing or even recognising

feelings, and connecting with emotions can be

challenging for adults.

Suppressing feelings can have an unpredictable effect on the body.

Learning to feel the emotion can bring about the growth of learning about oneself

and managing ones mental wellbeing.

Chew Yin created Curly and her friends to use as a tool to open up conversation

with our children, to encourage them to learn and talk about their feelings, to

ask questions about their feelings openly, rather than shut them away.

Building the bond and safe place to share for both carer and child.

Enjoy this fun book, which Chew Yin hopes will open up dialogue on why we

feel what we feel.

Remember there is no right or wrong way to feel, all feelings are valid based on

our perceptions.

Acknowledgments.

Sending much love and thanks to all who believed this book has a place in the education of self development from an early age. Who shared my passion for opening up a safe space between carer and child to explore emotions and accepting each other as we are, so we may bring out the best in one another.

Most of all, thank you to Curly for inspiring these book, based on your unconditional love for humans and the joy of exploring Hong Kong together.

 https://adventureswithcurlyandfriends.com/

 CurlyAndMonkey

 curlyandmonkey5